A HAIRCUT FO

by Connie Barreras
illustrations by Chris Sullivan

God is first. Family comes second. Everything else falls into place under those two things.

That is what makes life incredibly right and good.

I dedicate this book to my family, to the friends I've made over the years at the barber shop, and above all, to God.

— Barber Jon of World's Famous
 Barber Shop in El Dorado Hills, CA

Blessed are all who fear the Lord,
 who walk in obedience to him.

You will eat the fruit of your labor;
 blessings and prosperity will be yours.

Your wife will be like a fruitful vine
 within your house;

your children will be like olive shoots
 around your table.

Yes, this will be the blessing
 for the man who fears the Lord.

Psalm 128:1-4

Mr. Young saw it was time to go to the barber shop to get Henry's first 'real' haircut. "Come on, Henry," he said. "Let's go."

Henry pulled on his jacket slowly. "Will it hurt, Daddy?"

"Of course not, Henry, plenty of fellas' go to the barber shop. It feels nice to get a haircut. Plus, it's fun to hang out with the guys."

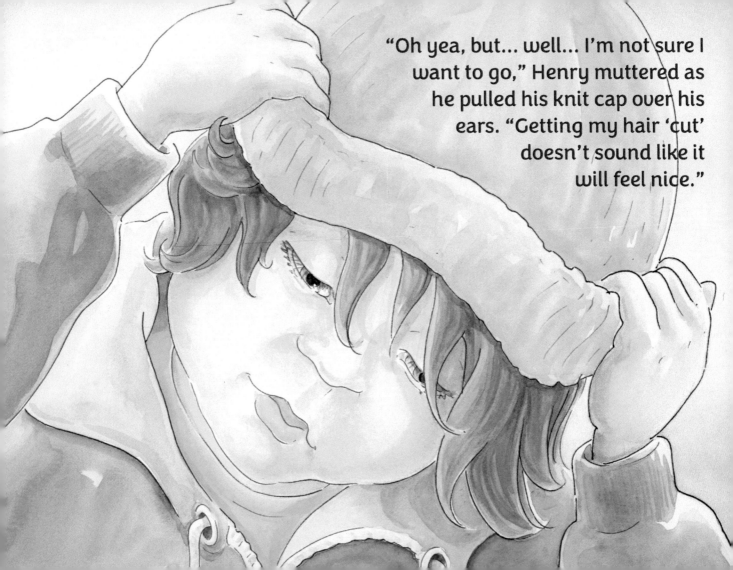

"Oh yea, but... well... I'm not sure I want to go," Henry muttered as he pulled his knit cap over his ears. "Getting my hair 'cut' doesn't sound like it will feel nice."

Henry was certain about one thing.
"This is NOT going to be a good day."

"Don't worry, you'll be fine," Mr. Young replied.
He took Henry's hand as they stepped out
onto the icy driveway to the truck.

They drove out of the neighborhood and headed up the hill.

BARBER JON'S

Whirl, Whirl, Whirl

Henry noticed a pole spinning outside as they pulled up to the barber shop. He climbed out of the car.

Whirl, Whirl, Whirl

spun the pole as the red, white and blue stripes traveled up and down.

As Mr. Young opened the shop door and then shut it behind Henry,

DING RING PING

the bells jingled.

Once inside, Henry saw several guys in the barbershop just like his daddy had said. A policeman and an older boy were sitting in green chairs. Henry sat down. His daddy picked up a nearby magazine.

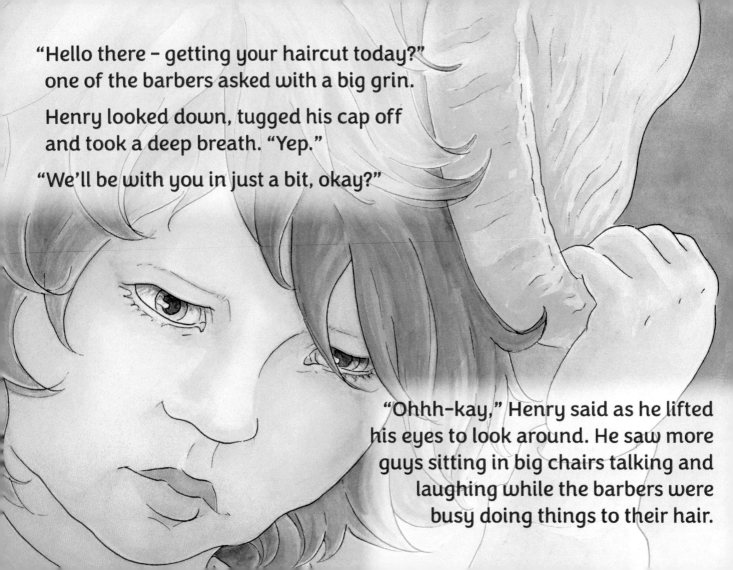

"Hello there – getting your haircut today?" one of the barbers asked with a big grin.

Henry looked down, tugged his cap off and took a deep breath. "Yep."

"We'll be with you in just a bit, okay?"

"Ohhh-kay," Henry said as he lifted his eyes to look around. He saw more guys sitting in big chairs talking and laughing while the barbers were busy doing things to their hair.

Henry sat and listened. None of the sounds he heard made Henry think that anybody was getting hurt. Relieved, Henry sighed and took another deep breath.

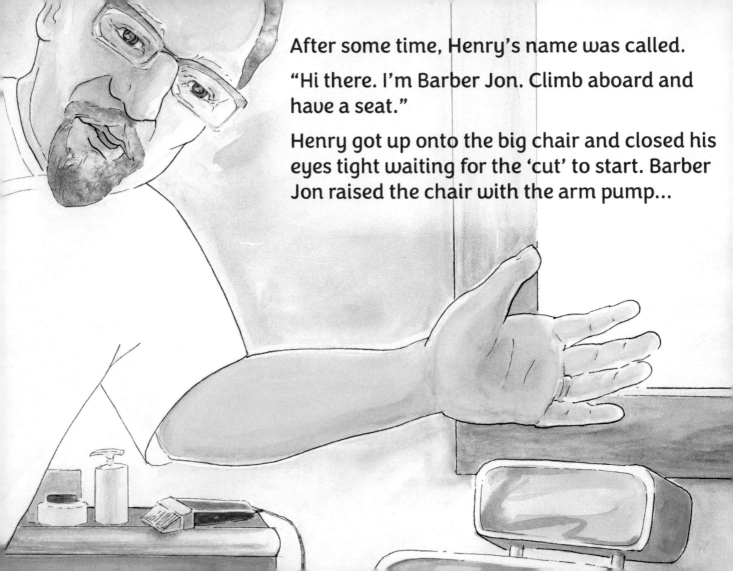

After some time, Henry's name was called.

"Hi there. I'm Barber Jon. Climb aboard and have a seat."

Henry got up onto the big chair and closed his eyes tight waiting for the 'cut' to start. Barber Jon raised the chair with the arm pump...

SHHWIRRT
SHHWIRRT
SHHWIRRT

...and the seat boosted
Henry higher and higher.
Henry's eyes popped open
to see what just happened!

Then Barber Jon spun a black cape around Henry.

whooooosh

He snapped it together around Henry's neck. "Your shirt won't get wet or hairy having this on," Barber Jon winked.

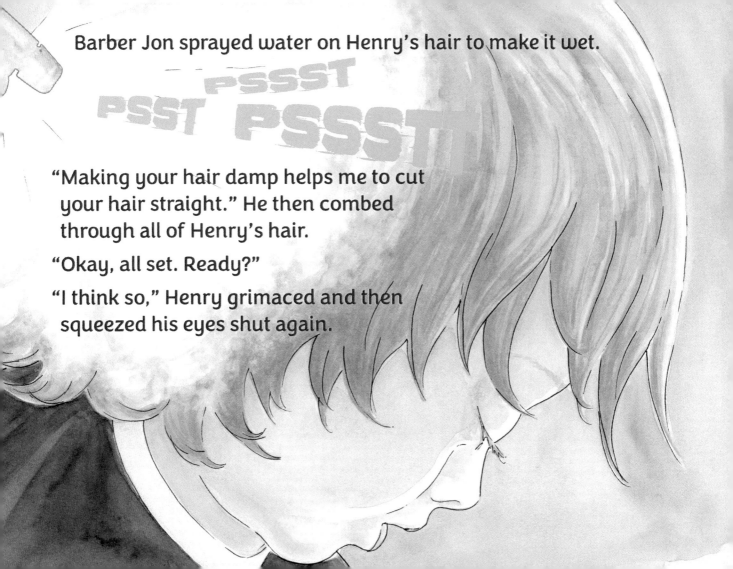

Barber Jon sprayed water on Henry's hair to make it wet.

PSSST
PSST PSSST

"Making your hair damp helps me to cut your hair straight." He then combed through all of Henry's hair.

"Okay, all set. Ready?"

"I think so," Henry grimaced and then squeezed his eyes shut again.

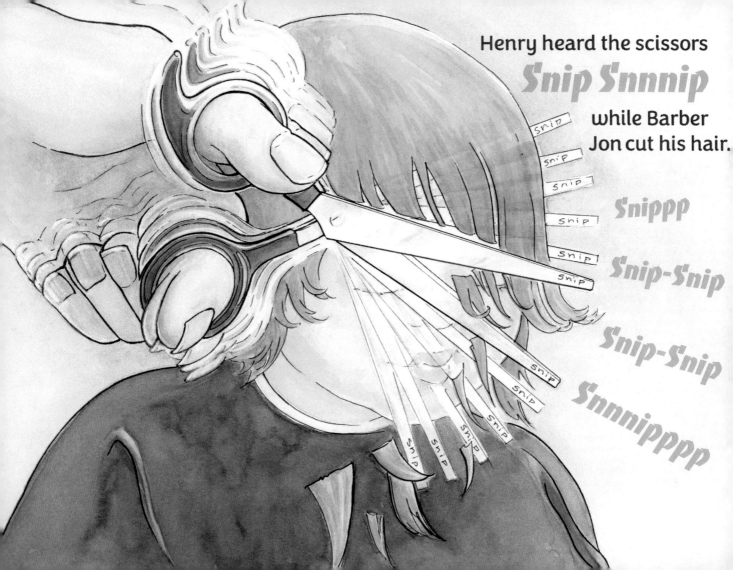

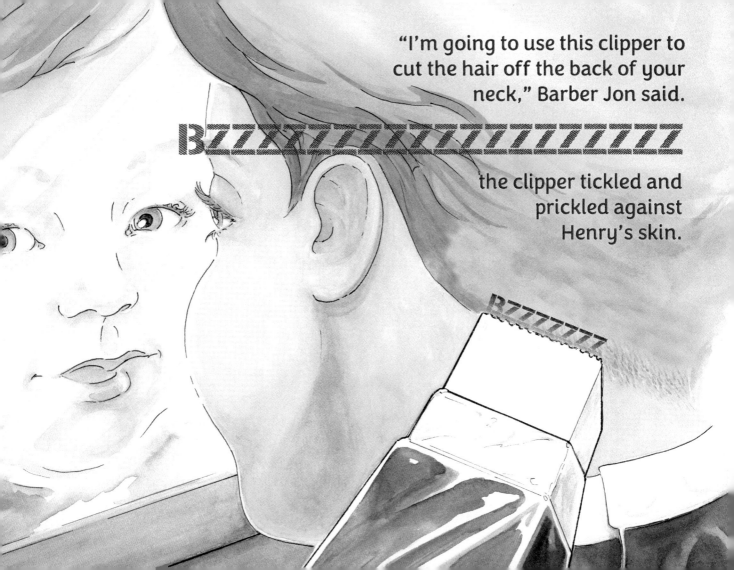

"I'm going to use this clipper to cut the hair off the back of your neck," Barber Jon said.

BZZZZZZZZZZZZZZZZZZZZZ

the clipper tickled and prickled against Henry's skin.

BZZZZZZZ

"And now, I think we're finished here, young man." Barber Jon spun Henry around as he aimed the hair dryer at Henry's head.

The warm air blew Henry's hair dry. Loose hairs on his neck and cape swirled into the air, then drifted to the floor.

Henry opened his eyes wide with surprise. That was fast, and it didn't even hurt!

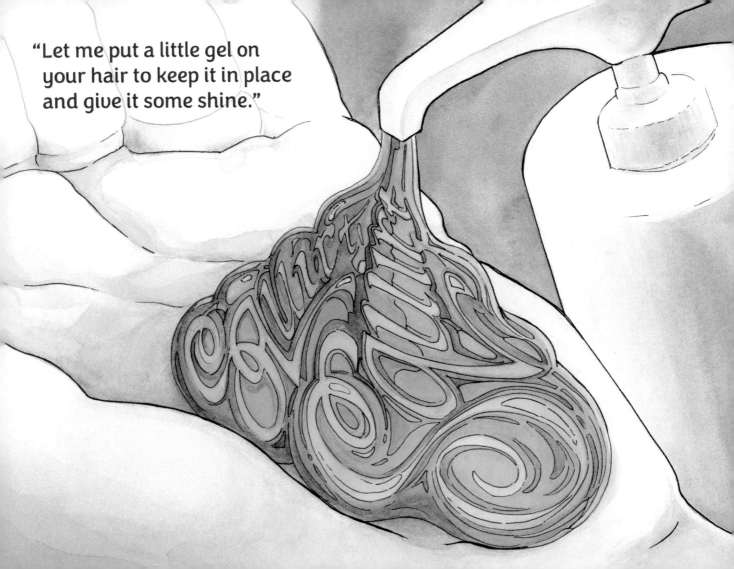

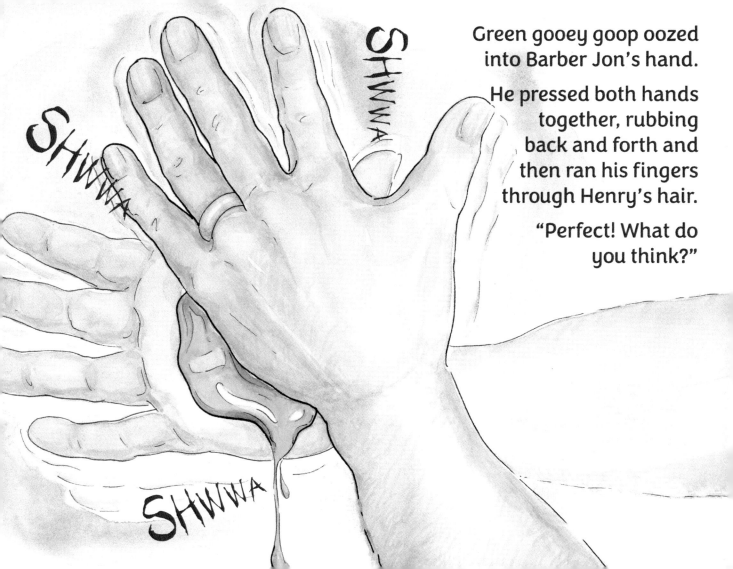

"I look different," Henry said
leaning toward the big mirror,
"But, I like it!"

"Yeah, it looks great, Henry,"
Mr. Young nodded.

"Get yourself a couple of gumballs in the machine by the door," Barber Jon pointed. He then began to sweep Henry's discarded hair from the floor.

Swisshh
Swisshh
Swisshh

Henry ran over to the giant gumball machine and turned the dial.
KER-PLUNK KER-PLUNK
A yellow and then a blue gumball fell into his hand.

KER-PLUNK

Henry popped both into his mouth as he followed his daddy outside.

Getting a haircut actually felt nice, Henry decided. It was going to be a good day after all.

MY FIRST OFFICIAL HAIRCUT

Certificate of Completion

presented to

_____

for a successful experience!

Date:_____

Location Name:_____

Signature and Name of Barber or Hairdresser:

_____

BEFORE PHOTO here: Tuft of Hair Here: AFTER PHOTO here:

Made in the USA
Columbia, SC
06 March 2022

57285728R00018